Truth in Charts

VOLUME 2

Aaron Erhardt

Erhardt Publications
Louisville, Kentucky
2015

Dedication

This book is dedicated to Kris Sanders,
who aspires to be a gospel preacher.

List of Charts

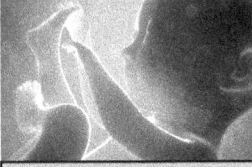

Abortion

Argument	Answer
A woman has a right to control her own body.	While it is true that a woman should control her own body, the baby's body is not her own. It is a different body with a genetic code that differs from the mother's. A woman's body does not have two hearts, heads, and blood types. And what if she is pregnant with a male child?
We cannot know if the fetus is a human being.	If that is so, shouldn't the benefit of the doubt go to preserving life? Scripture teaches and science affirms that the unborn are living human beings.
It is better to abort a child than abuse one.	Abortion is the worst form of child abuse. What could be more abusive than cutting someone into pieces or burning them with poison?
We cannot impose our morality on others.	Wouldn't this same argument apply to murder or rape? This nation was founded on morality. Those who make this argument are the very people trying to impose their immorality on others!
People are going to have abortions anyway.	Again, this same argument could apply to murder or rape. Because people are going to murder anyway, should we go ahead and legalize murder? Laws do affect behavior and change attitudes.
Rape victims should be able to abort the child.	The violence of abortion parallels the violence of rape. Why should the innocent child suffer the death penalty for the actions of his father? Abortion will not bring healing to the woman, it will only add to the shame. Also, less than 1% of abortions are performed as a result of rape.
You support the death penalty.	Capital punishment is rooted in respect for innocent human life. There is a vast difference between punishing a convicted murderer and killing an innocent child.

7 Sayings of Jesus on the Cross

"Father, forgive them, for they know not what they do." (Lk. 23:34)	• Jesus maintained a forgiving heart (Matt. 6:14-15) • Forgiveness is not granted in heaven until it is sought through obedience (Acts 2:38) • Stephen and Paul made similar statements (Acts 7:60; 2 Tim. 4:16)
"Truly, I say to you, today you will be with me in Paradise." (Lk. 23:43)	• "Paradise" refers to Hades (Acts 2:27, 31) • Hades is depicted in Luke 16:19-31 • The thief died before New Law took effect (Heb. 9:16-17)
"Woman, behold your son... Behold, your mother." (Jn. 19:26-27)	• This implies the death of Joseph • Fulfilled the fifth Commandment (Ex. 20:12) • Jesus made earthly provisions for His mother • No provisions were made for a wife (Paul named others, but not Jesus, when arguing for the right to have a wife)
"My God, my God, why you forsaken me?" (Matt. 27:46; Mk. 15:34)	• Quote from Psalm 22:1 • Psalm 22 graphically depicts the crucifixion (about 20 references) • Jesus was not asking a question in search of information; He was teaching • Jesus was not affirming the thoughts of unbelievers • Jesus would never be forsaken by the Father (Jn. 8:28-29; 16:32)
"I thirst." (Jn. 19:28)	• Shortest of seven • Stressed His humanity • Fulfillment of prophecy (Ps. 22:15; 69:12) • The One who created water and turned water into wine was thirsty
"It is finished." (Jn. 19:30)	• Old Law was nailed to the cross (Col. 2:14) • Satan's power of death destroyed (Heb. 2:14) • Purchase price for the church (Acts 20:28)
"Father, into your hands, I commit my spirit." (Lk. 23:46)	• Similar to Stephen (Acts 7:59) • Same words spoken by David (Ps. 31:5) • Jesus entrusted His spirit to the Father for safe keeping (into His care)

All four Gospel writers include at least one saying; none more than three. Luke records the first and last sayings — both addressed to the Father. The brevity would be typical of a victim of crucifixion.

Why Marriage?

(1) Partnership *(Gen. 2:18)*

(2) Procreation *(Gen. 1:28)*

(3) Purity *(1 Cor. 7:2)*

(4) Pleasure *(Song of Sol.)*

Marriage is an honorable estate. It was ordained by God in the garden of Eden and is the oldest institution in the world. Solomon declared, "He who finds a wife finds a good thing and obtains favor from the Lord" (Prov. 18:22).

Abraham's Obedience

"Take your son, your only son Isaac, whom you love, and go to the land of Moriah, and offer him there as a burnt offering..." (Gen. 22:2)

(1) No disputing. Abraham accepted the command without any argument or backtalk.

(2) No delaying. Abraham rose early in the morning to carry out the command.

(3) No disturbances. Abraham apparently did not tell his wife what he was doing, and kept the servants back from the site.

(4) No doubts. Abraham told the servants that they would both come back.

"He considered that God was able even to raise him from the dead..." (Heb. 11:19)

The Book of Genesis

Creation (Eden)

Corruption (Sin)

Catastrophe (Flood)

Confusion (Babel)

Commission (Abraham)

The Flood: Local or Universal?

(1) The Ark. There would have been no need for a vessel that size if it was a local flood. In fact, there would have been no need for a vessel at all.

(2) The Animals. There would have been no need to bring all the creatures aboard the ark if it was a local flood.

(3) The Birds. There would have been no need to send out birds to search for dry land if it was a local flood.

(4) The Rainbow. The bow in the cloud is a sign of the covenant God made with mankind to never again flood the world as He did. Yet there have been many local floods since that time.

(5) The Judgment. Peter compared the flood of Noah's day to the final judgment, which will certainly be universal.

Beautiful Women in the Bible

Sarai (Gen. 12:11, 14)

Rebekkah (Gen. 24:16; 26:7)

Rachel (Gen. 29:17)

Abigail (I Sam. 25:3)

Bathsheba (2 Sam. 11:2)

Tamar (2 Sam. 14:27)

Abishag (I Kgs. 1:4)

Vashti (Est. 1:11)

Esther (Est. 2:7)

Job's daughters (Job 42:15)

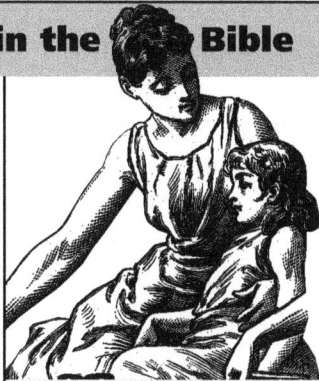

Though these women were very attractive outwardly, true beauty is found inwardly (1 Pet. 3:3-4).

Complaining

(1) **Condemned.** It angers God.

(2) **Controlling.** It becomes habitual.

(3) **Contagious.** It spreads to others.

(4) **Counter-productive.** It compounds the problem.

(5) **Conquerable.** It can be overcome.

"Do everything without complaining"
(Phil. 2:14, NCV)

Plagues on Egypt (Ex. 7-12)

(1) **River Plagues:** blood/frogs
(2) **Nuisance Plagues:** gnats/flies
(3) **Disease Plagues:** death of livestock/boils
(4) **Destruction Plagues:** hail/locusts
(5) **Darkness Plagues:** darkness/death of firstborn

• Outdoor morning confrontation: plagues 1, 4, 7 • Court confrontation: plagues 2, 5, 8 • No confrontation: plagues 3, 6, 9	The plagues were predicted, partial, and progressive

Outline of Joshua	
Crossing	The people of Israel cross the Jordan and enter Canaan.
Conquering	The people of Israel conquer the inhabitants of Canaan.
Claiming	The people of Israel divide the Land of Canaan.
The book of Joshua can also be outlined as "Conquest" (1-13:7) and "Settlement" (13:8-24)	

"Twos" in the Joseph Narrative

(1) Two dreams (Gen. 37:5, 9)

(2) Two confinements (Gen. 37:24; 39:20)

(3) Two advancements (Gen. 39:4, 22)

(4) Two lost coats (Gen. 37:23; 39:12)

(5) Two prisoners (Gen. 40:3)

(6) Two narrow escapes from death (Gen. 37:28; 39:20)

(7) Two dreams of Pharaoh (Gen. 41:1, 5)

David & Christ

Both were born in Bethlehem

Both were from lowly estates

Both were shepherds

Both were kings

Both brought victory

Both had a heart after God

Judah's Kings (Southern Kingdom)	Israel's Kings (Northern Kingdom)
Rehoboam — 17 years	Jeroboam I — 22 years
Jotham — 16 years	Jehu — 28 years
Abijam — 3 years	Nadab — 2 years
Ahaz — 16 years	Jehoahaz — 17 years
Asa — 41 years	Baasha — 24 years
Hezekiah — 29 years	Jehoash — 16 years
Jehoshaphat — 25 years	Elah — 2 years
Manasseh — 55 years	Jeroboam II — 41 years
Jehoram — 8 years	Zimri — 7 days
Amon — 2 years	Zechariah — 6 months
Ahaziah — 1 year	Tibni — 5 years
Josiah — 31 years	Shallum — 1 month
Athaliah — 6 years	Omri — 12 years
Jehoahaz — 3 months	Menahem — 10 years
Joash — 40 years	Ahab — 22 years
Jehoiakim — 11 years	Pekahiah — 2 years
Amaziah — 29 years	Ahaziah — 2 years
Jehoiachin — 3 months	Pekah — 20 years
Uzziah — 52 years	Jehoram — 12 years
Zedekiah — 11 years	Hoshea — 9 years

The good kings are highlighted.

* Not in chronological order

Eye Trouble

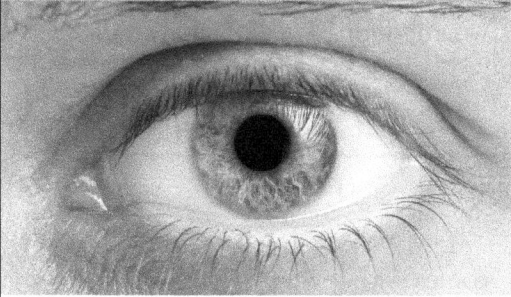

Eve **"saw"** that the tree was good for food (Gen. 3:6)

Lot **"saw"** that the land toward Sodom was good (Gen. 13:10)

Lot's wife **"looked back"** at the city (Gen. 19:26)

Potiphar's wife **"cast her eyes"** on Joseph (Gen. 39:7)

Achan **"saw"** the spoil (Josh. 7:21)

David **"saw"** Bathsheba taking a bath (2 Sam. 11:2)

"Oh, be careful little eyes what you see!"

Two Birth Announcements

Zechariah	Mary
Old	Young
Man	Woman
Temple	Home
Unbelief	Faith

There are several similarities in the announcements: both were troubled by the appearance of the angel, both were told not to be afraid, both were told they were having a son, both were told what to name their son, etc.

Pattern in Judges

Rebellion — forsake God	Sin
Retribution — oppressed	Slavery
Repentance — cry out	Supplication
Restoration — delivered	Salvation
Rest — enjoy peace	Silence

Premillennialism Timeline

	Rapture	Armageddon	Final Judgment
Church Age	Tribulation	Reign on Earth	
	(7 Years)	(1,000 Years)	
	Christ comes for saints	Christ comes with saints	Satan loosed for a season

Premillennial Order: silent rapture of saints — 7 year tribulation period — battle of Armageddon — 1,000 year reign of Christ — final judgment

Scriptural Order: second coming — resurrection of dead — final judgment

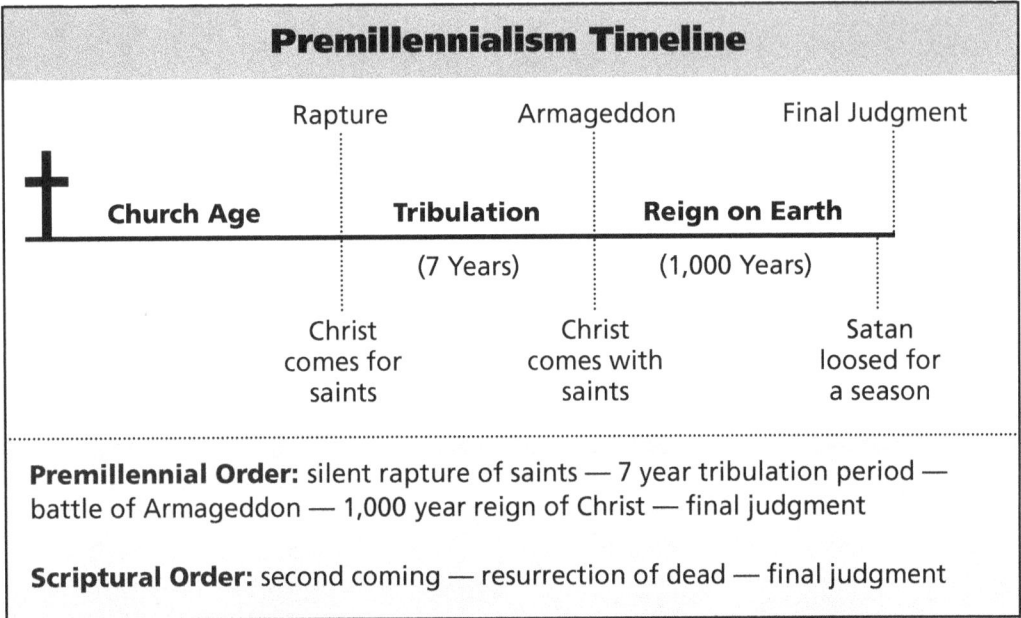

The Sign on the Cross

Matthew:
"This is Jesus, the King of the Jews"

Mark:
"The King of the Jews"

Luke:
"This is the King of the Jews"

John:
"Jesus of Nazareth, the King of the Jews"

Total:
"This is Jesus of Nazareth, the King of the Jews"

Was Peter the Pope?

(1) Peter never referred to himself as Pope.

(2) Peter was never referred to by others as Pope.

(3) The office of the papacy is not found in Scripture.

(4) Peter was "sent" by others on a mission in Acts 8.

(5) Peter was "opposed" by Paul in Galatians 2:11.

(6) James had the final say at meeting in Acts 15.

(7) Peter refused the praise of men in Acts 10.

(8) Peter was married and had children.

"Pope" comes from the Latin *papa*, meaning "father."

The Pope is called the "Vicar of Christ," meaning he presides in the place of Christ.

At the Feet of Jesus...

Mary, the sister of Martha and Lazarus, is seen three times in the Gospels. On each occasion she is at the feet of Jesus:

(1) "Mary, who sat at the Lord's feet and listened to his teaching" (Lk. 10:39)

(2) "Mary...fell at his feet, saying to him, 'Lord, if you had been here, my brother would not have died'" (Jn. 11:32)

(3) "Mary...anointed the feet of Jesus and wiped his feet with her hair" (Jn. 12:3)

The Great Image (Dan. 2)

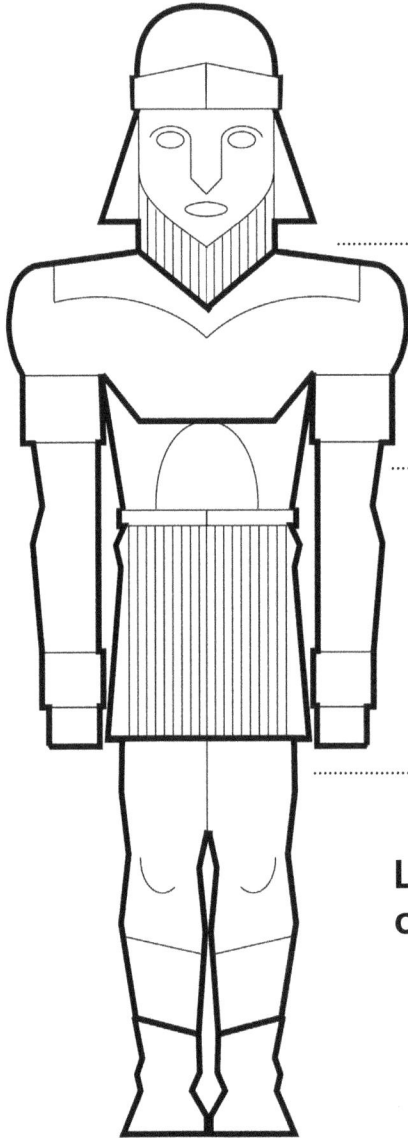

Head of Gold:
Babylonia
(626-539 B.C.)

**Chest/arms
of Silver:**
Medo-Persia
(539-330 B.C.)

**Middle/thighs
of Bronze:**
Greece
(330-63 B.C.)

**Legs of iron/feet
of Iron and Clay:**
Rome
(63 B.C.+)

Simeon (Lk. 2)

- **Pure:** .... "righteous and devout" (v. 25)
- **Patient:** .... "waiting for the consolation of Israel" (v. 25)
- **Preserved:** ... "would not see death before he had seen the Lord's Christ" (v. 26)
- **Prompted:** ... "he came in the Spirit into the temple" (v. 27)
- **Pleased:** .... "he took him up in his arms and blessed God" (v. 28)
- **Prophetic:** .... "this child is appointed for" (v. 34)

"Jeroboamitis" (1 Kgs. 12)

A selfish desire to substitute the Lord's way for your own way.

Wrong Standard	Heart
Wrong Motive	Selfish
Wrong Place	Dan/Bethel
Wrong People	Non-Levites
Wrong Time	15th Day/8th Month

Nicodemus (Jn. 3)

(1) **Strict:** Pharisee

(2) **Stately:** Ruler of the Jews

(3) **Secretive:** Came to Jesus by night

(4) **Searching:** Sought answers from Jesus

(5) **Shielding:** spoke up for Jesus (Jn. 7:51)

(6) **Sacrificial:** Brought large amount of expensive spices (Jn. 19:39)

> Nicodemus is mentioned three times in John's Gospel:
> - Visited Christ (ch. 3)
> - Defended Christ (ch. 7)
> - Honored Christ (ch. 19)

SILENCE: Permissive or Prohibitive?

- **1 Chronicles 17:6** — Silence prohibited David from building the Lord a new house.

- **Acts 15:24** — Silence prohibited Judaizers from binding circumcision on Gentiles.

- **Hebrews 7:14** — Silence prohibited Jesus from being a priest under the Old Law.

Post-Apostolic Period	Reformation Period	Restoration Period
In response to those who said that "the thing which is not forbidden is freely permitted," Tertullian declared, "I should rather say that what has not been freely allowed is forbidden."	Martin Luther initially taught that "whatever is without the word of God is, by that very fact, against God." However, he later stated, "What is not against Scripture is for Scripture, and Scripture for it." Ulrich Zwingli argued that practices "not enjoined or taught in the New Testament should be unconditionally rejected."	Thomas Campbell affirmed, "That with respect to the commands and ordinances of our Lord Jesus Christ, where the Scriptures are silent… no human authority has power to interfere." He even coined the cliché, "Where the Scriptures speak, we speak; Where the Scriptures are silent, we are silent."

God's silence speaks loudly! We are not to go beyond what is written (2 John 9).

Joseph of Arimathea

(1) **Prosperous:** "rich man" (Matt. 27:57)

(2) **Prominent:** "respected member of the Council" (Mk. 15:43)

(3) **Pure:** "good and righteous man" (Lk. 23:50)

(4) **Persuaded:** "a disciple of Jesus" (Matt. 27:57)

(5) **Pricked:** "took courage and went to Pilate" (Mk. 15:43)

(6) **Protective:** "laid it in his own new tomb" (Matt. 27:60)

Zacchaeus (Lk. 19)

(1) **Prestigious** — chief tax collector (v. 2)

(2) **Prosperous** — rich (v. 2)

(3) **Persistent** — ran ahead, climbed tree (v. 4)

(4) **Prompt** — hurried down, received him (v. 6)

(5) **Penitent** — restore it fourfold (v. 8)

(6) **Pardoned** — salvation came to house (v. 9)

Zacchaeus stands in contrast
to the rich ruler in the previous chapter. Zacchaeus
was willing to sacrifice material goods,
the rich ruler was not!

STOOPING SAVIOR

Jesus stooped to teach (Jn. 8:6, 8)

Jesus stooped to serve (Jn. 13:5)

Jesus stooped to pray (Lk. 22:41)

Jesus stooped to save (Phil. 2:5-8)

Personage of the Holy Spirit

Hears (Jn. 16:13)

Teaches (Jn. 14:26)

Comforts (Acts 9:31)

Leads (Rom. 8:14)

Loves (Rom. 15:30)

Knows (1 Cor. 2:11)

Communes (2 Cor. 13:14)

Speaks (1 Tim. 4:1)

Can be resisted (Acts 7:51)

Can be grieved (Eph. 4:30)

Can be quenched (1 Thess. 5:19)

Can be outraged (Heb. 10:29)

"Person:" a being characterized by conscious apprehension, rationality, and a moral sense.

Biblical Stonings

Blasphemer (Lev. 24:14)

Sabbath-breaker (Num. 15:36)

Achan (Josh. 7:25)

Abimelech (Jud. 9:53)

Naboth (1 Kgs. 21:10)

Stephen (Acts 7:58)

Paul (Acts 14:19)

SCOURGING

"It consisted of a handle, to which several cords or leather thongs were affixed, which were weighted with jagged pieces of bone or metal, to make the blow more painful and effective...The victim was tied to a post (Acts 22 25) and the blows were applied to the back and loins, sometimes even, in the wanton cruelty of the executioner, to the face and the bowels. In the tense position of the body, the effect can easily be imagined. So hideous was the punishment that the victim usually fainted and not rarely died under it"
(*International Standard Bible Encyclopedia*, Vol. 4, p. 2704).

"For they say that the bystanders were struck with amazement when they saw them lacerated with scourges even to the innermost veins and arteries, so that the hidden inward parts of the body, both their bowels and their members, were exposed to view"
(*Ecclesiastical History*, 4:15, p. 122).

The Beauty & The Beast	
Abigail	**Nabal**
Generous	Greedy
Hospitable	Hostile
Humble	Haughty
Selfless	Selfish
In 1 Samuel 25, Abigail heeded (vv. 14-17), hurried (vv. 18-20), humbled (vv. 23-31), halted (vv. 32-38), and hitched (vv. 39-42).	

Was Simon Saved?

The conversion of Simon in Acts 8 has been the source of much controversy. Some deny that he was really saved since his soul was in danger later in the chapter. However, the evidence indicates that Simon was saved.

(1) The Lord's statement in Mark 16:16. Jesus said that whoever believes and is baptized will be saved. Simon did that.

(2) The phrase "even Simon himself believed." This indicates that his belief was the same as the others in Samaria.

(3) The phrase "he continued with Philip." This indicates that he was recognized by Philip and the other disciples as a faithful brother.

(4) The command to "repent and pray." This is the second law of pardon for erring Christians. Those never saved must repent and be baptized (Acts 2:38).

What I See in the Cross

(1) The love of God *(Jn. 3:16)*

(2) The humility of Christ *(Phil. 2:6-8)*

(3) The value of man *(Rom. 5:6-8)*

(4) The means of peace *(Eph. 2:14-16)*

(5) The removal of Old Law *(Col. 2:14)*

(6) The truth of prophecy *(Jn. 19:24, 28, 36)*

(7) The cost of discipleship *(Matt. 16:24)*

Attempts to "Bury" Resurrection

ARGUMENT	ANSWER
The body was stolen. Either the disciples or grave robbers took the corpse.	(1) The tomb was secured with a large stone and soldiers. (2) Thieves would not take the time to unwrap the body in the tomb.
Jesus did not die. He regained consciousness in the tomb and left. This is sometimes called the "swoon theory."	(1) The body was examined by Joseph, Nicodemus, and soldiers who were experienced in crucifixion. They all concluded that He was dead. (2) A severally beaten, crucified, and speared man could not move the large stone and sneak past the soldiers.
The disciples went to the wrong place. They mistakenly went to an empty tomb.	(1) Several disciples were present at the burial, including Joseph, Nicodemus, and two Marys. (2) All the naysayers would have to do is go to the right tomb and produce the body.
The disciples were hallucinating. This was caused by an ardent expectation of His resurrection.	There were many post-resurrection appearances of Jesus, including 500 people at one time.

3 "noble" qualities of the "noble" Bereans	(1) **They had an open heart.** They received the word eagerly.
	(2) **They had an open Bible.** They examined the Scriptures to see.
	(3) **They had an open schedule.** They made time to study daily.

CRUCIFIXION

"The suffering of death by crucifixion was intense, esp. in hot climates. Severe local inflammation, coupled with an insignificant bleeding of the jagged wounds, produced traumatic fever, which was aggravated by the exposure to the heat of the sun, the strained position of the body and insufferable thirst. The wounds swelled about the rough nails and the torn and lacerated tendons and nerves caused excruciating agony. The arteries of the head and stomach were surcharged with blood and a terrific throbbing headache ensued. The mind was confused and filled with anxiety and dread foreboding. The victim of crucifixion literally died a thousand deaths. Tetanus not rarely supervened and the rigors of the attending convulsions would tear at the wounds and add to the burden of pain, till at last the bodily forces were exhausted and the victim sank into unconsciousness and death" (*International Standard Bible Encyclopedia*, Vol. 2, p. 761).

"What prevents me from being baptized?" (Acts 8:36)	
	(1) Ignorance. Some people don't know that baptism is essential to salvation.
	(2) Embarrassment. Some people feel uncomfortable being baptized with others watching.
	(3) Misconceptions. Some people have the wrong idea about who should be baptized.
	(4) Misplaced Loyalties. Some people refuse baptism because their loved ones were not baptized.

Saved on the Road?

If Saul of Tarsus was saved on the road to Damascus...

The Lord did not know it. He told Saul to enter the city where he would be told what to do (Acts 9:6).

Saul did not know it. He was miserable until he was baptized a few days later (Acts 9:9, 18-19).

Ananias did not know it. He told Saul to be baptized and wash away his sins (Acts 22:16).

Luke and the Holy Spirit did not know it. They record that he was still in his sins until baptism (Acts 22:16).

What Saul "saw" during his blindness (Acts 9:9)

(1) Saul saw that he was a sinner.

(2) Saul saw that his father's religion was wrong.

(3) Saul saw that his conscience was not a safe guide.

(4) Saul saw that Jesus and the church are inseparable.

(5) Saul saw that prayer does not save alien sinners.

(6) Saul saw that there was something to do.

The Bible	Calvinism
"The gospel, it is the power of God for salvation" (Rom. 1:16)	"The direct operation of the Holy Spirit, it is the power of God for salvation"
"Faith comes from hearing, and hearing through the word of Christ" (Rom. 10:17)	"Faith comes from the direct operation of the Holy Spirit"
"He brought us forth by the word of truth" (Jam. 1:18)	"He brought us forth by the direct operation of the Holy Spirit"
"The implanted word, which is able to save your souls" (Jam. 1:21)	"The direct operation of the Holy Spirit, which is able to save your souls"
"You have been born again through the living and abiding word of God" (1 Pet. 1:23)	"You have been born again through the direct operation of the Holy Spirit"
"He called you through our gospel" (2 Thess. 2:14)	"He called you through the direct operation of the Holy Spirit"
"Those who believe in me through their word" (Jn. 17:20)	"Those who believe in me through the direct operation of the Holy Spirit"

Paul said that it was when the Ephesians "heard" and "believed" that they were "sealed" with the Holy Spirit (Eph. 1:13). Calvinists, on the other hand, say that man is sealed with the Holy Spirit before he can hear and believe!

Why People Do Not Examine the Scriptures Today (Acts 17:11)

(1) **Distracted.** They are focused on other ideas, books, things, etc.

(2) **Disillusioned.** They are turned off by all the division, scandals, etc.

(3) **Dishonest.** They are wedded to error no matter what.

(4) **Discouraged.** They are overwhelmed by the Bible.

(5) **Disinterested.** They just don't care.

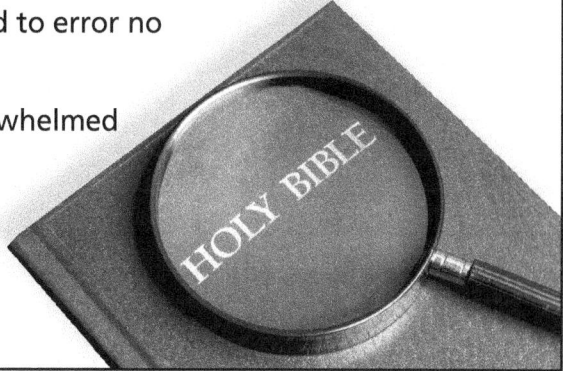

Now It Is Different...

the hiscox standard BAPTIST MANUAL
EDWARD T. HISCOX

A stunning quote from the Standard Manual for Baptist Churches:

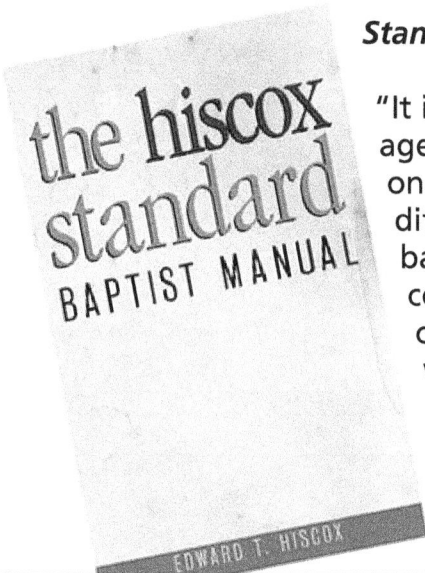

"It is most likely that in the Apostolic age when there was but 'one Lord, one faith, and one baptism,' and no differing denominations existed, the baptism of a convert by that very act constituted him a member of the church and at once endowed him with all the rights and privileges of full membership. In that sense, 'baptism was the door into the church.' Now it is different..." (E.T. Hiscox).

How Do You See Christ?

Martin Luther: "And all the prophets saw this, that Christ was to become the greatest thief, murderer, adulterer, robber, desecrator, blasphemer, etc., there has ever been anywhere in the world. He is not acting in His own Person now. Now He is not the Son of God, born of the Virgin. But He is a sinner..." (*Luther's Works*, Galatians 3:13, p. 277).

Christ died for our sins, but He did not make them His own. He was not a sinner. He was a perfect lamb "without blemish or spot" (1 Pet. 1:19). He was not what Luther saw!

Tongue Speaking Regulations

According to 1 Corinthians 14	
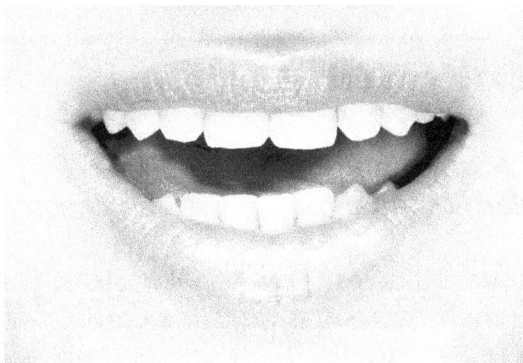	(1) No more than two or three (v. 27)
	(2) They must take turns (v. 27)
	(3) They must have an interpreter (v. 27)
	(4) Women must remain silent (v. 34)

Compare these "divine regulations" to what takes place within holiness churches today. Do they limit the number of tongue speakers to two or three? Do they take turns? Do they have an interpreter? Do they tell women to keep silent? They defy the regulations set in place by the very Spirit they claim is leading them!

Old Baptists & Reverend (1)

"Some of the words used by the Baptists of today in their preaching, writing, and conversation are altogether alien to the verbiage of the early Christians. Who could image Onesimus going to Philemon and talking to him about 'The Reverend Paul?' Who could imagine Gaius writing to the 'Reverend John' to give him a good report about the 'Reverend Demetrius?' Yet modern Baptists use the term 'Reverend' every day in speaking of preachers or writing about them...If the Baptists of the medieval age could hear it today they would cry against the use of this title which has been borrowed from an ecclesiastical hierarchy that would draw a line between the laity and the ministry. When the word 'Reverend' is used in the Bible, it refers to God, for He alone is to be revered" (*Baptist Standard*, Editorial Section, p. 2, April 9, 1955).

Old Baptists & Reverend (2)

"The term Reverend, now in such common use among our people and all other parties, was generally very offensive to Baptists of the old school, and was seldom employed by them in common conversation, in letter inscriptions, or in any other way. Holy and Reverend is his name, as a designation of the Divine Being, was a passage often quoted by objectors to giving reverence to men. To the Deity alone, said they, reverence belongs" (*50 Years Among the Baptists*, David Benedict, p. 286).

GRACE

The God of grace (1 Pet. 5:10)
The throne of grace (Heb. 4:16)
The Spirit of grace (Heb. 10:29)
The word of grace (Acts 20:32)
The Son "full" of grace (Jn. 1:14)

Witnesses of the Resurrection

(1) The **volume** of witnesses. The more witnesses you have, the stronger your testimony. Jesus was seen by over 500 people at one time, in addition to others.

(2) The **variety** of witnesses. Some who saw Jesus had not previously believed (his brothers), some were skeptical (Thomas), and some were outright enemies (Saul).

(3) The **veracity** of witnesses. Those who saw Jesus were bold in their testimony, even to the point of death. They knew what they saw and would not be silenced.

7 Churches of Asia (Rev.2-3)

Ephesus: sound but shallow

Smyrna: poor but rich

Pergamum: strong but weak

Thyatira: loving but lax

Sardis: living but dead

Philadelphia: weak but strong

Laodicea: rich but poor

5 Spiritual Conditions

SAFE	SEPARATED	SAVED	SEVERED	SALVAGED
Innocent	Guilty	Forgiven	Fallen	Restored

Hymanaeus

(1) **His crime.** False teaching (2 Tim. 2:18)

(2) **His calculation.** Swerved from the truth (2 Tim. 2:18)

(3) **His condition.** Faith shipwrecked (1 Tim. 1:19)

(4) **His casualties.** Led others astray (2 Tim. 2:18)

(5) **His cohorts.** Alexander and Philetus (1 Tim. 1:20; 2 Tim. 2:17)

(6) **His consequences.** Handed over to Satan (1 Tim. 1:20)

"Hymenaeus" was named after Hymen, the god of marriage.
He lived in Ephesus and is mentioned twice in Scripture
(1 Tim. 1:20; 2 Tim. 2:17). The fact that he is named first may
indicate that he was the leader.

A Christian Is...

A believer (1 Thess. 1:7)

A son of God (Gal. 3:26)

A disciple (Acts 11:26)

A priest (Rev. 1:6)

A saint (Phil. 1:1)

A soldier (2 Tim. 2:3)

A servant (Gal. 1:10)

A light (Phil. 2:15)

The term "Christian" appears three times in the New Testament (Acts 11:26; 26:28; 1 Pet. 4:16). It refers to one who belongs to and follows after Christ.

GRACE	MERCY
When God gives us what we don't deserve	When God doesn't give us what we do deserve

Salvation by grace proves that man lacks ability, not accountability. It proves the salvation is undeserved, not unconditional!

Jesus at the Raising of Lazarus (Jn. 11)

(1) **Comradery.** He was a friend (vv. 3, 5, 11, 36).

(2) **Courage.** He returned to dangerous Judea (vv. 7-16).

(3) **Comfort.** He assured Martha of resurrection (vv. 23-26).

(4) **Compassion.** He felt deep emotion (vv. 33, 35, 38).

(5) **Command.** He ordered Lazarus to come out (vv. 43-44).

OLD LAW	NEW LAW
Old (2 Cor. 3:14)	New (2 Cor. 3:6)
Abolished (Heb. 10:9)	Established (Heb. 10:9)
By Prophets (Heb. 1:1)	By Christ (Heb. 1:2)
To Jews (Gen. 17:13)	To Every Creature (Mk. 16:15)
Shadow (Col. 2:17)	Substance (Col. 2:17)
Offerings Repeated (Heb. 10:11)	Christ Once Offered (Heb. 7:27)
Sins Remembered (Heb. 10:3)	Sins Forgotten (Heb. 8:12)

Old Baptists & Instruments

"Staunch old Baptists in former times would as soon have tolerated the Pope of Rome in their pulpits as an organ in their galleries, and yet the instrument has gradually found its way among them…" (*50 Years Among the Baptists*, David Benedict, p. 283).

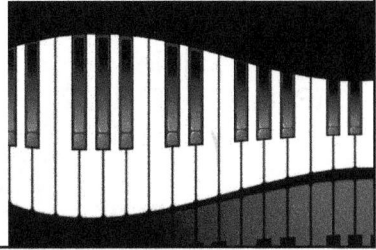

Hospitality

Exhortations	Examples
Rom. 12:13 "…seek to show hospitality"	Abraham (Gen. 18) Lot (Gen. 19) Jethro (Ex. 2) The Samaritans (Jn. 4) Martha (Lk. 10) Zaccheus (Lk. 19) Simon (Acts 9) Cornelius (Acts 10) Philip (Acts 21) Gaius (3 John)
Heb. 13:2 "Do not neglect to show hospitality…"	
1 Pet. 4:9 "Show hospitality to one another…"	

Jesus on hospitality: "Truly, I say to you, as you did to one of the least of these my brothers, you did it to Me" (Matt. 25:40).

How Faith Comes (A Parallel)

Acts 15:7	*Romans 10:17*
By my mouth	By hearing
Word of the Gospel	Word of Christ
Believe	Faith

The Lord's Army

Occupation
Soldier
(Phil. 2:25; Phile. 2; 2 Tim. 2:3-4)

Opponent
The devil
(Eph. 6:11, 16; 1 Pet. 5:8)

Objective
To stand
(Eph. 6:11, 13, 14; Phil. 4:1)

Orders
Put on armor of God
(Eph. 6:11, 13, 14-17)

NOTS

Bible: "Whoever believes and is baptized will be saved"

Baptists: "Whoever believes and is NOT baptized will be saved"

Bible: "Baptism, which corresponds to this, now saves you"

Baptists: "Baptism, which corresponds to this, NOT saves you"

The Amazing Grace of God

(1) **Grace** saves (Eph. 2:8)

(2) **Grace** calls (2 Tim. 1:9)

(3) **Grace** justifies (Tit. 3:7)

(4) **Grace** trains (Tit. 2:12)

(5) **Grace** strengthens (Heb. 13:9)

"Grace" is unmerited favor or undeserved blessing. It can be summed up as "not receiving what we deserve and not deserving what we receive."

Divine Verification of OT

On numerous occasions, Jesus gave testimony to the historicity of Old Testament people and stories.

Solomon and his wealth (Matt. 6:29)

David and the showbread (Matt. 12:3-4)

Jonah and the great fish (Matt. 12:39-41)

Queen of Sheba and wisdom of Solomon (Matt. 12:42)

Adam and Eve (Matt. 19:4-5)

Slaying of Abel and Zechariah (Matt. 23:35)

Noah and the flood (Matt. 24:37-39)

Elijah and the drought (Lk. 4:25-26)

Elisha and Naaman (Lk. 4:27)

Patriarchs and prophets (Lk. 13:28)

Lot, his wife, and the destruction of Sodom (Lk. 17:28-32)

Lifting up of bronze serpent (Jn. 3:14)

Moses and the manna (Jn. 6:32, 49)

Elders

"Pay careful attention to yourselves and to all the flock, in which the Holy Spirit has made you overseers, to care for the church of God, which he obtained with his own blood" (Acts 20:28)

Divine Position: "Holy Spirit has made you overseers"

Divine People: "The church of God"

Divine Price: "He obtained with his own blood"

3 Portraits of Philip the Evangelist

Helper	Herald	Host
"Therefore, brothers, pick out from among you seven men of good repute, full of the Spirit and of wisdom, whom we will appoint to this duty... and they chose... Philip" **Acts 6:3, 5**	"Philip went down to the city of Samaria and proclaimed to them the Christ... Then Philip opened his mouth, and beginning with this Scripture he told him the good news about Jesus" **Acts 8:5, 35**	"On the next day we departed and came to Caesarea, and we entered the house of Philip the evangelist, who was one of the seven, and stayed with him" **Acts 21:8**

5 Things the Jehovah's Witnesses Deny...

(1) The personality of the Holy Spirit

(2) The eternality of Jesus Christ

(3) The immortality of man

(4) The existence of hell

(5) The end of earth

The Jehovah's Witnesses is a religious organization founded by Charles Taze Russell (1852-1916), though the name was not adopted until 1931.

Greek Terms	English Words	Emphasis
Poimen	Shepherd, Pastor	Feed, Guard
Episcopos	Overseer, Bishop	Inspect, Watch
Presbuteros	Elder, Presbyter	Experience, Maturity

Too Spiritual a Fibre?

"Although Josephus tells of the wonderful effects produced in the Temple by the use of instruments, the first Christians were of *too spiritual a fibre* to substitute lifeless instruments for or to use them to accompany the human voice"
(*Catholic Encyclopedia*, Vol. 10, p. 651, emp. mine).

If the first Christians were of "too spiritual a fibre" to use mechanical instruments in worship, what does that say about those who use them in worship today?

The Model Prayer (Matt. 6)

Address the Father	"Our Father in heaven" (v. 9)
Offer praises to His name	"Hallowed be your name" (v. 9)
Offer petitions for kingdom	"Thy kingdom come" (v.10)
Offer petitions for needs	"Give us this day our daily bread" (v.11)
Offer petitions for forgiveness	"Forgive us our debts" (v.12)
Offer petitions for deliverance	"Deliver us from evil" (v.13)

The kingdom came in Acts 2.
However, the principle of praying for the kingdom remains.

Evolution

- Assumes that all things came about by chance.

- Assumes that life came about from non-life.

- Has an effect without an adequate cause.

- Has no explanation for moral conscience.

Theory: About 13.7 billion years ago a tiny singularity (smaller than a proton) exploded resulting in inflation, which led to the material universe.

Response: This theory cannot explain where the tiny singularity came from, or how a tiny singularity exploding could produce such a massive explosion. The very idea violates the "Law of Cause and Effect," which says every material effect must have an adequate cause that existed before the effect.

Ants in Your Pants

"Sloth" is laziness. It can denote either inactivity or sluggishness in the performance of a task. Words like "apathy," "idleness," "indifference," and "lethargy" are often associated with sloth. A slothful person delays work and does not complete work already begun. He cuts corners and looks for the easy way out.

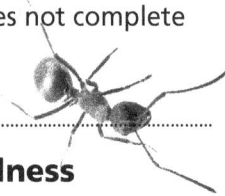

Proverbs on Slothfulness

"As vinegar to the teeth, and as smoke to the eyes, so is the slothful to those sending him" (10:26).

"The soul of the slothful is desiring, and hath not. And the soul of the diligent is made fat" (13:4).

"The way of the slothful is as a hedge of briers, and the path of the upright is raised up" (15:19).

"The slothful hath hidden his hand in a dish, even unto his mouth he bringeth it not back" (19:24; also 26:15).

"Because of winter the slothful plougheth not, he asketh in harvest, and there is nothing" (20:4).

"The desire of the slothful slayeth him, for his hands have refused to work" (21:25).

"The slothful hath said, 'A lion is without, in the midst of the broad places I am slain'" (22:13; also 26:13).

"The door turneth round on its hinge, and the slothful on his bed" (26:14).

"Wiser is the slothful in his own eyes, than seven men returning a reason" (26:16).

"Go unto the ant, O slothful one, See her ways and be wise; Which hath not captain, overseer, and ruler, She doth prepare in summer her bread, She hath gathered in harvest her food. Till when, O slothful one, dost thou lie? When dost thou arise from thy sleep? A little sleep, a little slumber, A little clasping of the hands to rest, And thy poverty hath come as a traveller, And thy want as an armed man" (Proverbs 6:6-11, YLT).

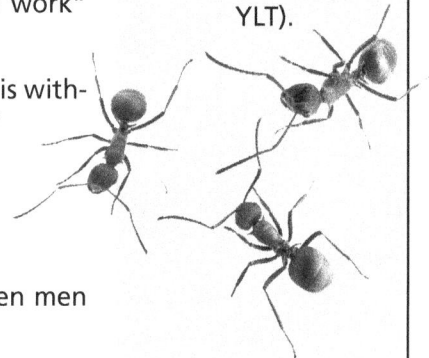

"Twisting to their own destruction" (2 Pet. 3:16)

Bible: baptized — wash away sins — calling **Men:** calling — wash away sins — baptized	"Rise and be baptized and wash away your sins, calling on his name" (Acts 22:16)
Bible: repent — baptized — forgiveness of sins **Men:** repent — forgiveness of sins — baptized	"Repent and be baptized...for the forgiveness of your sins" (Acts 2:38)
Bible: believe — baptized — saved **Men:** believe — saved — baptized	"Whoever believes and is baptized will be saved" (Mk. 16:16)

Church Fathers on Free Will

Justin Martyr: "We maintain that each man acts rightly or sins by his free choice."

Melito: "There is, therefore, nothing to hinder you from changing your evil manner of life, because you are a free man."

Irenaeus: "Man...having been made free in his will, and with power over himself, is himself his own cause that sometimes he becomes wheat, and sometimes chaff."

Clement of Alexandria: "It is by one's own fault that he does not choose what is best. God is free of blame."

Tertullian: "Man is free, with a will either for obedience or resistance."

Origen: "Every rational soul has free will and volition...we are not forced by any necessity to act either rightly or wrongly."

— *Quotes taken from A Dictionary of Early Christian Beliefs, pp. 285-289*

Scripture teaches that man has a free will: "I have set before you life and death... choose life" (Deuteronomy 30:19); "Choose this day whom you will serve" (Joshua 24:15); "They...did not choose the fear of the Lord" (Proverbs 1:29); "If you are willing and obedient...but if you refuse and rebel" (Isaiah 1:19-20); "Enter by the narrow gate" (Matthew 7:13); "Come to me" (Matthew 11:28); "Come to me and drink" (John 7:37); "Save yourselves" (Acts 2:40); "Work out your own salvation" (Philippians 2:12); "Choosing rather to be mistreated with the people of God" (Hebrews 11:25); etc. Furthermore, Jesus said the people of Jerusalem "would not" come (Matthew 23:37), not "could not" come. Obviously, man has a choice!

10 Strikes Against Calvinistic Predestination

"Calvinistic Predestination" says God arbitrarily chose a certain fixed number of individuals to be saved before the foundation of the world and condemned everyone else. This limits the scope of His grace, love, and mercy to a few (and not all). Compare that idea to Scripture:

Christ invited "all" to come (Matt. 11:28)

Christ said preach to "whole creation" (Mk. 16:15)

Gospel offers salvation to "everyone" (Rom. 1:16)

Christ died for "all" (2 Cor. 5:14)

God wishes that "all" reach repentance (2 Pet. 3:9)

Christ is the propitiation for sins of the "whole world" (1 Jn. 2:2)

God wants "all" to be saved (1 Tim. 2:4)

Christ gave Himself as a ransom for "all" (1 Tim. 2:6)

Grace appeared for "all" people (Tit. 2:11)

Christ tasted death for "everyone" (Heb. 2:9)

"Calvinistic Predestination" makes God a respecter of persons, which He is not (Acts 10:34; Rom. 2:11; Eph. 6:9). God predestined the plan, not the man. Everyone who chooses to accept the gospel can be saved!

Lover of Money?

Signs:

Feel you never have enough

Feel the need to flaunt it

Feel resentment giving it

Will sin to get it

Examples:

Achan (Josh. 7)

Gehazi (2 Kgs. 5)

Judas Iscariot (Matt. 26)

Ananias and Sapphira (Acts 5)

"The love of money is a root of all kinds of evils" (1 Tim. 6:10)

"Keep your life free from love of money" (Heb. 13:5)

"A dreadful thing is the love of money! It disables both eyes and ears, and makes men worse to deal with than a wild beast, allowing a man to consider neither conscience nor friendship nor fellowship nor salvation" (Chrysostom)

Church of Christ "Before" Campbell

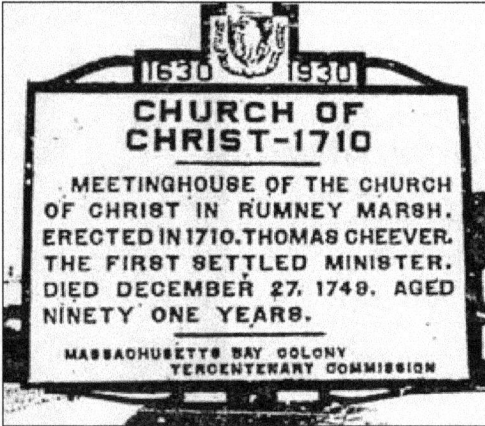

CHURCH OF CHRIST–1710

MEETINGHOUSE OF THE CHURCH OF CHRIST IN RUMNEY MARSH. ERECTED IN 1710. THOMAS CHEEVER. THE FIRST SETTLED MINISTER. DIED DECEMBER 27, 1749. AGED NINETY ONE YEARS.

MASSACHUSETTS BAY COLONY TERCENTENARY COMMISSION

Some people claim that Alexander Campbell started the church of Christ. Though this can easily be disproven from Scripture (Rom. 16:16), there are many historical arguments to be made as well. For instance, this marker says there was a church of Christ in Rumney Marsh, Massachusetts in 1710. Campbell was not born until 1788 and did not come to America until 1809.

Other historical arguments include a tombstone at the Cane Ridge Meetinghouse ("united with the church of Christ at Cane Ridge in 1807") and a marker at the Old Mulkey Meetinghouse ("1809...they aspired to be the church of Christ that is written about in the Bible"). Campbell did not come to Kentucky until 1823.

Ekklesia

Etymological Meaning
"ek" out + "kaleo" to call = the called out.
It refers to people who are called out
of the world to God.

Everyday Meaning
"Ekklesia" was not an inherently religious word.
It was used for any group assembled for a purpose
(Acts 19:32, 39, 41).
It was used for Christ's assembly:
universal (Matt. 16:18) and local (Matt. 18:17).
It was never used for a building.
"Ekklesia" refers to people, not places!

King James ordered that ecclesiastical words be kept in his translation. This included the word "church," even though it is derived from the Greek *kuriake*, and not *ekklesia* (see edict 3).

Origin of the Baptist Church

"The history of Baptist churches cannot be carried, by the scientific method, farther back than the year 1611, when the first Anabaptist church consisting wholly of Englishmen was founded in Amsterdam by John Smyth, the Se-Baptist. This was not, strictly speaking, a Baptist Church, but it was the direct progenitor of churches in England that a few years later became Baptist, and therefore the history begins there" (*A Short History of the Baptists,* p. 4).

"The word Baptists, as the descriptive name of a body of Christians, was first used in English literature, so far as is known, in the year 1644... There had been no such churches before, and hence there was no need of the name" (*Ibid.,* p. 3).

"The earliest instance in which this name occurs as a denominational designation, so far as my information goes, befell in the year 1644... The name Baptist was in 1644 first claimed by our people. They have claimed it ever since" (*A Question in Baptist History,* pp. 92-93).

We want to be in the Lord's church of the first century, not John Smyth's church of the seventeenth century!

Follow the Rules!

1 Chronicles 15:13:
"Because you did not carry it the first time, the Lord our God broke out against us, because we did seek him *according to the rule*"
(ESV, emp. mine).

KJV: "after the due order"

RSV: "in the way that is ordained"

NIV: "in the prescribed way"

NASB: "according to the ordinance"

NLV: "in the way He had told us"

Message: "We didn't...follow instructions"

AMP: "in the way He ordained"

GW: "in the way he designated"

LEB: "according to the law"

Growth in Acts

2:41 "there were added that day about three thousand souls"
2:47 "the Lord added to their number day by day"
4:4 "the number of men came to about five thousand"
5:14 "more than ever believers were added to the Lord"
5:14 "multitudes of both men and women"
6:1 "the disciples were increasing in number"
6:7 "the number of the disciples multiplied greatly"
8:12 "they were baptized both men and women"
9:31 "the church...multiplied"
9:42 "many believed in the Lord"
11:21 "a great number who believed turned to the Lord"
11:24 "a great many people were added to the Lord"
12:24 "the word of God increased and multiplied"
13:49 "the word of the Lord was spreading throughout the whole region"
14:1 "a great number of both Jews and Gentiles believed"
14:21 "had made many disciples"
16:5 "they increased in numbers daily"
17:4 "some of them were persuaded and joined Paul and Silas"
17:4 "a great many of the devout Greeks and not a few of the leading women"
17:34 "some men joined him and believed"
18:8 "many of the Corinthians believed and were baptized"

* This list does not include some of the individual conversions

Capital Punishment

- Rooted in respect for human life (Gen. 9:6)
- Incorporated in the Old Law (Num. 35:16-21)
- Authorized in the New Law (Rom. 13:4)
- Some crimes merit death (Acts 25:11)
- Should be carried out swiftly (Eccl. 8:11)

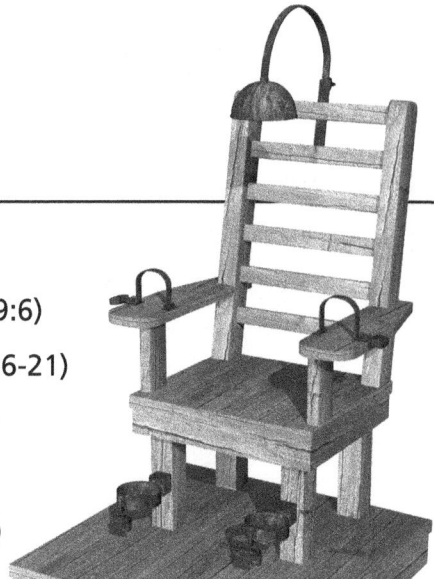

Jesus on Divorce

Matt. 5:32
"But I say to you that everyone who divorces his wife, except on the ground of sexual immorality, makes her commit adultery, and whoever marries a divorced woman commits adultery."

Matt. 19:9
"And I say to you: whoever divorces his wife, except for sexual immorality, and marries another, commits adultery."

Jesus gave only one reason for divorce!

Stand Firm...

...in the faith (1 Cor. 16:13)

...in the freedom (Gal. 5:1)

...in the Lord (Phil. 4:1)

...in the grace (1 Pet. 5:12)

A Baptist Preacher on Falling Away

At Least He is Consistent!

"We take the position that a Christian's sins do not damn his soul. The way a Christian lives, what he says, his character, his conduct, or his attitude toward other people have nothing whatever to do with the salvation of his soul...All the prayers a man may pray, all the Bibles he may read, all the churches he may belong to, all the services he may attend, all the sermons he may practice, all the debts he may pay, all the ordinances he may observe, all the laws he may keep, all the benevolent acts he may perform will not make his soul one whit safer; and all the sins he may commit from idolatry to murder will not make his soul in any more danger...The way a man lives has nothing whatever to do with the salvation of his soul"

(Does A Christian's Sins Damn His Soul? Sam Morris, tract).

The Lord's Day

Didache (90 A.D.) — "And on the Lord's own day gather yourselves together and break bread" (14:1)

Barnabas (100 A.D.) — "We keep the eighth day [Sunday] with rejoicing, in the which also Jesus rose from the dead" (15:9)

Justin (150 A.D.) — "And on the day called Sunday, all who live in cities or in the country gather together to one place… Sunday is the day on which we all hold our common assembly" (Apology, 68)

Justin (150 A.D.) — "We do not live according to the Law…nor do we observe the Sabbath as you do" (Dialogue, 10:1)

Tertullian (200 A.D.) — "By us, to whom Sabbaths are strange" (Idolatry, 14:6)

Cyprian (250 A.D.) — "The eighth day…the Lord's Day" (Epistle 58)

Ignatius (250 A.D.) — "At the dawning of the Lord's day He arose from the dead…The day of the preparation, then, comprises the passion; the Sabbath embraces the burial; the Lord's day contains the resurrection" (Trallians, 9)

Ignatius (250 A.D.) — "Let every friend of Christ keep the Lord's day as a festival, the resurrection day" (Magnesians, 9)

Eusebius (300 A.D.) — "They did not, therefore, regard circumcision nor observe the Sabbath; neither do we… because such things as these do not belong to Christians" (Ecclesiastical History, 1:4)

John's Three Epistles

1 John:
Fellowship with God

2 John:
Fellowship with false teachers (none)

3 John:
Fellowship with those who teach truth

Plan of Salvation in Romans

Hear (Rom. 10:17)

Believe (Rom. 1:16)

Repent (Rom. 2:4)

Confess (Rom. 10:10)

Baptized (Rom. 6:3)

Campbell or Christ?

This is the tombstone of William Rogers. It is located on the grounds of the Cane Ridge Meetinghouse in Bourbon County, Kentucky.

The tombstone says that Rogers was "united with the church of Christ at Cane Ridge in 1807." That is significant since Alexander Campbell did not come to America until 1809 and did not visit Kentucky until 1823.

Alexander Campbell: "I have no idea of adding to the catalogue of new sects. I labor to see sectarianism abolished…" (*Christian Baptist*, 1826)

NRSV Preface on "Jehovah"

"The form 'Jehovah' is of late medieval origin; it is a combination of the consonants of the Divine Name and the vowels attached to it by the Masoretes but belonging to an entirely different word… The word 'Jehovah' does not accurately represent any form of the Name ever used in Hebrew."

יְהֹוָת

Constantine

Though Constantine may have been one of the greatest emperors in Roman history, his impact on the church was for the worst. He secularized and paganized the church. He adopted his own model rather than trying to restore the one of the New Testament.

272 A.D. Constantine was born to Flavius Constantus and Helena. She was a Bithyian woman of low social status.

303 A.D. Constantine was married to Minervina (303-307).

307 A.D. Constantine was married to Fausta (307-326).

312 A.D. Constantine won the "Battle of the Milvian Bridge." He claimed to have seen a cross of light in the sky with an inscription that said, "In this sign, you will conquer."

313 A.D. Constantine and his co-emperor Licinius issued the "Edict of Milan," which legalized Christianity in the empire.

320 A.D. Constantine exempted Christian leaders from paying taxes.

321 A.D. Constantine decreed that Sunday was a day of rest in the empire.

324 A.D. Constantine defeated Licinius in a civil war and moved the capital to ancient site of Byzantium. It was called "New Rome" and then "Constantinople."

325 A.D. Constantine convened the "First Council of Nicea."

337 A.D. Constantine died in Nicomedia.

Alexander Campbell Timeline

1788 Born in Ireland to Thomas and Jane Campbell

1808 Shipwrecked on way to America; attended Glasgow University in Scotland

1809 Arrived in America

1810 Formation of Brush Run Church

1811 Married Margaret Brown

1812 Birth of first child; baptized by immersion in Buffalo Creek

1820 Debated John Walker (Presbyterian) on baptism

1823 Debated W. L. Maccalla (Presbyterian) on baptism; began Christian Baptist

1826 Published The Living Oracles, a translation of the New Testament

1827 Death of Margaret Brown

1828 Married Selina Bakewell

1829 Debated Robert Owen (skeptic) on evidences of Christian faith

1830 Relations with Baptists officially terminated; began Millennial Harbinger

1837 Debated John Purcell (Catholic Bishop) on Roman Catholicism

1840 Founded Bethany College

1843 Debated Nathan Rice (Presbyterian) on baptism, Holy Spirit, and creeds

1849 Formation of the American Christian Missionary Society

1850 Addressed both Houses of Congress

1866 Died in Bethany at home

The Civil War began in 1861

Power in the Blood

It frees
(Rev. 1:5)

It cleanses
(1 Jn. 1:7)

It justifies
(Rom. 5:9)

It redeems
(Eph. 1:7)

It sanctifies
(Heb. 13:12)

It reconciles
(Rom. 5:10)

It makes peace
(Col. 1:20)

It forgives sin
(Matt. 26:28)

One contacts the blood in baptism (Rom. 6:3; compare Matt. 26:28 and Acts 2:38). Furthermore, the church was "obtained" (ESV) or "purchased" (KJV) with the blood (Acts 20:28).

The Bible: Providentially Preserved

"The word of the Lord remains forever."

(1 Peter 1:25)

- The Scriptures were written on perishable material and had to be copied by hand for several thousand years.

- The Roman Emperor Diocletian (303 A.D.) ordered all copies of the Scriptures to be burned.

- The Roman Catholic Church burned thousands of copies of the Scriptures under the guise that the translation was vulgar.

- Voltaire, a French philosopher, actively sought to destroy faith in the Scriptures with his writings. He predicted that within one hundred years of his death, the Bible and Christianity would be extinct.

Why Is It?

- **WHY IS IT** that criminals have been prosecuted for killing unborn children in an attack on a pregnant woman but the mother could kill the child without penalty?

- **WHY IS IT** that we show more concern for speckled owls and rain forests than we do for human life?

- **WHY IS IT** that a rapist cannot be executed for his crime but the child conceived in the act can be executed?

- **WHY IS IT** that we hold a mother responsible for her unborn child's condition when she abuses drugs or alcohol but do nothing when she kills the child through abortion?

- **WHY IS IT** that many in our society oppose the death penalty for guilty criminals but will march on the streets of Washington for the rights of women to execute innocent babies?

- **WHY IS IT** that a nation which prides itself on humanitarianism treats its most helpless citizens (unborn babies) so in humanely?

- **WHY IS IT** that a person who picks up the egg of a preborn bald eagle can be severly punished by law (see Bald Egg Protection Act) but the same person can legally destroy a preborn child?

Ronald Reagan on Abortion

"I have often said that when we talk about abortion, we are talking about two lives — the life of the mother and the life of the unborn child. Why else do we call a pregnant woman a mother? I have also said that anyone who doesn't feel sure whether we are talking about a second human life should clearly give life the benefit of the doubt. If you don't know whether a body is alive or dead, you would never bury it. I think this consideration itself should be enough for all of us to insist on protecting the unborn"
(quoted from *Silenced Cries: A Study of Abortion*, p. 53).

Sword of the Spirit

Draws (Jn. 6:44-45)

Sanctifies (Jn. 17:17)

Produces Faith (Rom. 10:17)

Cleanses (Eph. 5:26)

Encourages (1 Thess. 4:18)

Teaches (2 Thess. 2:15)

Calls (2 Thess. 2:14)

Reproves (2 Tim. 3:16)

Saves (Jam. 1:21)

Purifies (1 Pet. 1:22)

Produces Birth (1 Pet. 1:23)

Produces Growth (1 Pet. 2:2)

"...the sword of the Spirit, which is the word of God"
(Eph. 6:17)

Overseers in the Church

Service
- Flock-feeding (1 Pet. 5:2)
- Example-setting (1 Pet. 5:3)
- Soul-watching (Heb. 13:17)
- Self-heeding (Acts 20:28)
- Mouth-stopping (Tit. 1:11)

Selection
- Spirit-made (Acts 20:28)
- Church-selected (Acts 6:1-6)
- Preacher-appointed (Tit. 1:5)

"The Outward Appearance"

When measuring members.
They are often deemed "faithful" by outward appearances, such as attendance, public participation, and how nice they dress.

When measuring preachers.
They are often deemed "great" by outward appearances, such as speaking ability, number of converts, and level of education.

When measuring elders.
They are often deemed "qualified" by outward appearances, such as age, marital situation, and number of children.

When measuring churches.
They are often deemed "strong" by outward appearances, such as the building, number of members, and amount of contribution.

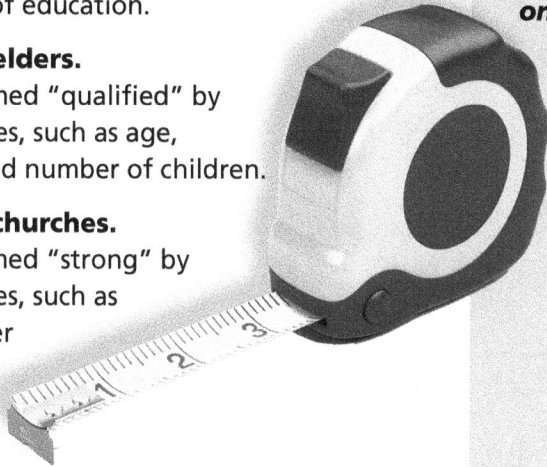

"For the Lord sees not as man sees; man looks on the outward appearance, but the Lord looks on the heart"
I Sam. 16:7

3 Kinds of Responses

Some Balk.
They are not interested.

NO

Some Talk.
They are willing to have dialogue.

MAYBE

Some Walk.
They are ready to commit

YES

"Now when they heard of the resurrection of the dead, some mocked. But others said, 'We will hear you again about this.' So Paul went out from their midst. But some men joined him and believed..."
Acts 17:32-34

David vs. Goliath (I Sam. 17)

David's Disadvantages

AGE	"You are only a boy, and he's been a man of war since his youth... this ruddy-faced boy" (vv. 33, 42)
ARMOR	"He wore a bronze helmet, and his bronze coat of mail weighed 125 pounds. He also wore bronze leg armor... His armor bearer walked ahead of him carrying a shield" (vv. 5-6, 7)
ARTILLERY	"He carried a bronze javelin on his shoulder. The shaft of his spear was as heavy and thick as a weaver's beam, tipped with an iron spearhead that weighed 15 pounds" (vv. 6-7)
ATHLETICISM	"Then Goliath, a Philistine champion from Gath... champion... champion" (vv. 4, 23, 51)
ANATOMY	"He was over nine feet tall" (v. 4)

What Baptism "Will" and "Will Not" Do

Baptism WILL	Baptism WILL NOT
Save (I Pet. 3:21)	Save alone
Forgive past sins (Acts 2:38)	Forgive future sins
Put one in Christ (Gal. 3:27)	Keep one in Christ
Place one in the body (I Cor. 12:13)	Place one in a denomination
Effect salvation (Mk. 16:16)	Merit salvation

BIBLE

COMPELLED
(driven into existence)
- 2 Tim. 3:16 – "breathed out"
- 2 Pet. 1:21 – "carried along"

COMPLETE
(final and perfect)
- Jn. 16:13 – "all the truth"
- Jude 3 – "once for all delivered"

COMPREHENSIBLE
(knowable)
- Jn. 8:32 – "you will know the truth"
- Eph. 3:4 – "you can perceive my insight"

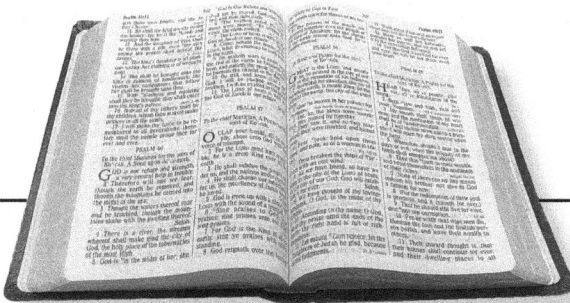

PARABLES

DEFINITION:
"Parable" literally means "to cast alongside." It is an earthly story that teaches heavenly truths. It is intended to both reveal and conceal.

DANGER:
Some people ignore important features of the parable, while others try to make every detail mean something.

SOWER

Hardened Heart:
fell along the path.
The close-minded person

Shallow Heart:
fell on rocky ground.
The impulsive person

Crowded Heart:
fell among thorns.
The preoccupied person

Sincere Heart:
fell on good soil.
The genuine person

The Seed:
the Word of God
The Sower:
the one who spreads the Word
The Soil:
the different conditions of man's heart

That's the Book for Me!

The Bible is a library of 66 books
(39 books in OT and 27 books in NT)

The Bible was written over a span of 1600 years
(1500 BC – 100 AD)

The Bible was written in three languages
(Hebrew, Aramaic, and Greek)

The Bible was written by more than 40 writers
(Shepherds, statesmen, fishermen, tax collectors, etc.)

The Bible proves itself to be the Word of God
(accuracy, fairness, prophecy, preservation, etc.)

Inquiring or Instructing?

Jesus was not *inquiring* (asking a question in search of information);
He was *instructing* (quoting a Scripture to teach the people).

- Jesus quoted Psalm 22:1, which graphically described the crucifixion scene. He wanted them to see that the psalm was being fulfilled.
- Jesus promised that He would never be forsaken by the Father, even during the crucifixion (Jn 8:28-29; 16:32).
- The people considered Jesus to be God-forsaken. He was not affirming their thoughts; He was seeking to correct their thoughts.
- There was no reason for Jesus to be forsaken by the Father. He was "a lamb without blemish or spot" (I Pet. 1:19). Jesus took away our sins, but did not take on our sins (i.e., make them His own).

"My God, my God, why have you forsaken Me?"
Matt. 27:46

From the Garden to Glory

RESTRAINED.	REPUDIATED.	REJECTED.
Jesus arrested	Jesus denied	Barabbas chosen
(Matt. 26:47-57)	(Matt. 26:69-75)	(Matt. 27:15-26)
	REVILED.	RESURRECTED.	
	Jesus mocked	Jesus raised	
	(Matt. 27:27-44)	(Matt. 28:1-8)	

There is something in your hair!

14:6 – He "ripped the lion's jaws apart with his bare hands. He did it as easily as if it were a young goat."

14:19 – He "went down to the town of Ashkelon, killed thirty men, took their belongings, and gave their clothing to the men who had solved his riddle."

15:8 – He "attacked the Philistines with great fury and killed many of them."

15:14 – He "snapped the ropes on his arms as if they were burnt strands of flax, and they fell from his wrists."

15:15 – He "found the jawbone of a recently killed donkey. He picked it up and killed 1,000 Philistines with it."

16:3 – He "took hold of the doors of the town gate, including the two posts, and lifted them up, bar and all. He put them on his shoulders and carried them all the way to the top of the hill across from Hebron."

16:9 – He "snapped the bowstrings as a piece of string snaps when it is burned by a fire."

16:12 – He "snapped the ropes from his arms as if they were thread."

16:14 – He "pulled back the loom shuttle, and yanked his hair away from the loom and the fabric."

16:29-30 – He "put his hands on the two center pillars that held up the temple. Pushing against them with both hands, he prayed, 'Let me die with the Philistines.' And the temple crashed down on the Philistine rulers and all the people."

"If my head were shaved, my strength would leave me, and I would become as weak as anyone else"

Judges 16:17, NLT

There is no indication that Samson looked like a weightlifter. He was an ordinary looking person with extraordinary power.

The Twelve (Matt. 10:1-4)

Peter	His name always appears first in the list of apostles. He was originally called "Simon." He was the leader of the group, often acting as their spokesman. He was the son of John and brother of Andrew. He was a fisherman by trade. He had a wife and served as an elder.
Andrew	He introduced his brother Peter to Jesus. He was the first of John's disciples to follow Jesus. He was a fisherman by trade.
James	He was the son of Zebedee and brother of John. He was the first apostle to die. He was martyred by Agrippa I. He and his brother were nicknamed "sons of thunder" by Jesus. He was a fisherman by trade.
John	He was the brother of James and wrote five books in the Bible. He was the last apostle to die. He referred to himself as "the disciple whom the Lord loved."
Philip	He was from Bethsaida and introduced Nathanael to Jesus.
Batholomew	He was called "Nathanael" in John's Gospel. He was declared to have "no deceit" by Jesus.
Thomas	He was called "the Twin" in John's Gospel. He may have been Matthew's twin since they are coupled in all three lists of the apostles in the Gospels.
Matthew	He was originally called "Levi." He was the son of Alphaeus. He was a tax collector and wrote the Gospel of Matthew.
James	He was called "the Younger" in Mark's Gospel.
Thaddaeus	He was called "Judas the son of James" in Luke's Gospel and in Acts.
Simon	He was called "the Zealot" in Luke's Gospel.
Judas Iscariot	His name always appears last in the lists of the apostles. He was the son of Simon. He held the moneybag for Jesus. He betrayed the Lord and committed suicide.

Renata Sedmakova / Shutterstock.com

Waterless Springs of Theology

"But false prophets also arose among the people, just as there will be false teachers among you… These are waterless springs"
(2 Pet. 2:1, 17)

A "waterless spring" is useless. It is all show but no substance. It promises what it cannot produce. Jude had the same idea in mind when he spoke of "waterless clouds" (v. 12). These false doctrines appear refreshing, but will ultimately leave you wanting!

(1) **Faith alone.**
Man is justified by faith (Rom. 5:1), but not by faith alone (Jam. 2:24). He must obey to be saved (Matt. 7:21).

(2) **Earthly kingdom.**
The kingdom was to be established during the days of the Roman Empire (Dan. 2:44). It was at hand in John's day (Matt. 3:2). It was established in the first century (Col. 1:13).

(3) **Once saved, always saved.**
While a believer does not come into judgment (Jn. 5:24), he can become an unbeliever (Heb. 3:12). It is possible to fall away (Gal. 5:4), depart from the faith (1 Tim. 4:1), turn back (2 Pet. 2:21), etc.

(4) **Latter-day revelation.**
The Spirit led the apostles into all the truth (Jn. 16:13). The faith was once for all delivered (Jude 3).

(5) **No literal hell.**
Jesus spoke of hell more than anyone else (11 times). It is a place you go (Mk. 9:43). It is a much worse punishment than death (Heb. 10:29).

Nicodemus / Woman at the Well

John 3	John 4
Man	Woman
Jew	Samaritan
Moral	Immoral
Regarded	Low Repute

Judging

Without judging, we could never answer these questions:

- Who are the "dogs" and "pigs" (Matt. 7:6)?

- Who are the "false prophets" (Matt. 7:15)?

- Who is to be "avoided" (Rom. 16:17)?

- Who is "caught in a transgression" (Gal. 6:1)?

- Who is "walking in idleness" (2 Thess. 3:6)?

- Who is "persisting in sin" (1 Tim. 5:20)?

- Who is "stirring up division" (Tit. 3:10)?

- Who is "wandering from the truth" (Jam. 5:19)?

- Who is "not abiding in the teaching of Christ" (2 Jn. 9)?

- Who is "bringing in destructive heresies" (2 Pet. 2:1)?

Jesus condemned hypocritical judging in Matthew 7, but commanded right judging in John 7.

"Judge with righteous judgment" *(Jn. 7:24)*

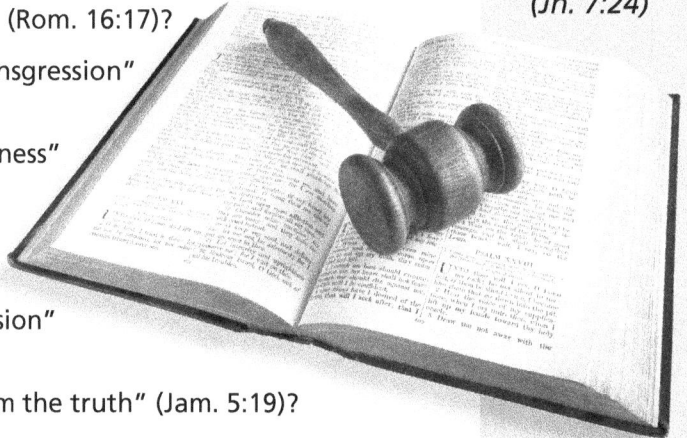

"Judge not, that you be not judged" *(Matt. 7:1)*

God Is...

"God is true" (Jn. 3:33)

"God is spirit" (Jn. 4:24)

"God is one" (Rom. 3:30)

"God is faithful" (I Cor. 1:9)

"God is able" (2 Cor. 9:8)

"God is not mocked" (Gal. 6:7)

"God is not unjust" (Heb. 6:10)

"God is a consuming fire" (Heb. 12:29)

"God is light" (I Jn. 1:5)

"God is love" (I Jn. 4:16)

"White" Lies

She was told when the Lord will return.
"... we heard the voice of God like many waters, which gave us the day and hour of Jesus' coming" (A Word to the Little Flock, p. 14). *Compare that to Matthew 24:36.*

The blood of Christ was not to cancel sin.
"the blood of Christ, while it was to release the repentant sinner from the condemnation of the law, was not to cancel sin" (Patriarchs and Propehts, p. 357) *Compare that to Matthew 26:28 & Epheisans 1:7.*

Enoch was taught by Noah.
"Enoch first received instruction from Noah, and he observed the law of God, and served him with singleness of heart" (The Review and Herald, April 29, 1875). *Enoch was translated to heaven long before Noah was born.*

Jesus was not God.
"The man Chirst Jesus was not the Lord God Almighty" (Letter 32, 1899, quoted in the Seventh-day Adventist Bible Commentary, Vol. 5, p. 1129). *Compare that to Isaiah 9:6.*

Paul learned the gospel from men in the church.
"Jesus directs him to His agents in the church for a further knowledge of duty. Thus He gives authority and sanction to His organized church. Christ had done the work of revelation and conviction, and now Paul was in a condition to learn of those whom God had ordained to teach the truth... The very men whom Paul was purposing to destroy were to be his instructors in the very religion that he had despised and persecuted" (Testimonies for the Church, Vol. 3, p. 430). *Compare that to Galatians 1:11-12.*

Ellen G. White was a co-founder of the Seventh-day Adventist Church. She claimed to have the "spirit of prophecy."

There is no eternal torment for the wicked.
"It is beyond the power of the human mind to estimate the evil which has been wrought by the heresy of eternal torment... The theory of eternal torment is one of the false doctrines that constitute the wine of the abominations of Babylon" (The Great Controversy, p. 536). *Compare that to Matthew 25:46.*

There is a temple in the Holy City.
"I saw an angel flying swiftly to me. He quickly carried me from the earth to the Holy City. In the city I saw a temple, which I entered" (The Early Writings, p. 32). *Compare that to Revelation 21:22.*

The plan of salvation was made after the fall.
"The kingdom of grace was instituted immediately aftr the fall of man, when a plan was devised for the redemption of the guilty race" (The Great Controversy, p. 347). *Compare that to Ephesians 1:4 and 3:10-11.*

The Father has a body.
"The Father is all the fullness of the Godhead bodily, and is invisible to mortal sight" (Evangelism, p. 614). *God is a spirit, which does not have flesh and bones (John 4:24; Luke 24:39). She inserted "The Father" in place of "Christ" (Colossians 2:9).*

25 Things a Child of God Can Do...

1) Be cut off (Rom. 11:22)

2) Be disqualified (1 Cor. 9:27)

3) Believe in vain (1 Cor. 15:1-2)

4) Be severed from Christ (Gal. 5:4)

5) Fall away from grace (Gal. 5:4)

6) Shift from the hope (Col. 1:23)

7) Be taken captive (Col. 2:8)

8) Depart from the faith (1 Tim. 4:1)

9) Stray after Satan (1 Tim. 5:15)

10) Swerve from the faith (1 Tim. 6:21)

11) Fall away from the living God (Heb. 3:12)

12) Be hardened by the deceitfulness of sin (Heb. 3:13)

13) Fail to reach the promise (Heb. 4:1)

14) Fall by the same sort of disobedience (Heb. 4:11)

15) Spurn the Son of God (Heb. 10:29)

16) Profane the blood of the covenant (Heb. 10:29)

17) Outrage the Spirit of grace (Heb. 10:29)

18) Throw away their confidence (Heb. 10:35)

19) Fail to obtain the grace of God (Heb. 12:15)

20) Become defiled (Heb. 12:15)

21) Refuse him who speaks from heaven (Heb. 12:25)

22) Be led away by diverse and strange teachings (Heb. 13:9)

23) Fall under condemnation (Jam. 5:12)

24) Wander from the truth (Jam. 5:19)

25) Deny the Master (2 Pet. 2:1)

Old Baptists & "eis"

"Finally, suppose we force eis in Acts ii. 38 to bear the unnatural and unauthorized meaning of 'on account of.' After all we have gained nothing. Other passages there are which cannot be explained away. Thus our Savior said, just before he ascended the heavens: He that believeth and is baptized shall be saved. We shall hardly dare to tamper with his royal word and make it run, He that believeth and is saved shall be baptized. And unless we do thus change his saying, we have, by the highest authority, an importance attributed to Baptism certainly not less than that given to it in Acts ii. 38, translated, according to its obvious meaning. What then is the advantage of violently torturing eis, the construction and the context?

We conclude without hesitation and in accordance with such authorities as Hackett, Winer, Meyer, etc., that the proper rendering eis aphesin hamartion in Acts ii. 38, as in Matthew xxvi. 28, is unto, for, i.e., IN ORDER TO, Remission of Sins" (*Baptism and Remission*, J.W. Willmarth, p. 306, July 1877).

www.ingramcontent.com/pod-product-compliance
Lightning Source LLC
Chambersburg PA
CBHW081241020426
42331CB00013B/3258